Toasts

for

Every
Occasion

D0051453

Town&Country

Toasts
for
Every
Occasion

. . .

FOREWORD BY
Pamela Fiori

INTRODUCTION BY
Francine Maroukian

ILLUSTRATIONS BY
John Ueland

. . .

Hearst Books
A Division of Sterling Publishing Co., Inc.
New York

Text copyright © 2004 by Hearst Communications, Inc.

Illustrations © 2004 by John Ueland

The Library of Congress has cataloged the hardcover edition as follows:
Town & country toasts for every occasion / foreword by Pamela Fiori :
introduction by Francine Maroukian : illustrations by John Ueland.
p.cm.
Includes bibliographical references and index.
ISBN 1-58816-393-8
1. Toasts. I. Title: Town and country toasts for every occasion.
II. Maroukian, Francine.
PN6341.T69 2004
808.5'1—dc22

2003023398

10 9 8 7 6 5 4 3 2 1

Book design by Celia Fuller
First Paperback Edition 2007

Published by Hearst Books
A Division of Sterling Publishing Co., Inc.
387 Park Avenue South, New York, NY 10016

www.townandcountrymag.com

For information about custom editions, special sales, premium and
corporate purchases, please contact Sterling Special Sales Department at
800-805-5489 or specialsales@sterlingpub.com.

Distributed in Canada by Sterling Publishing
^c/o Canadian Manda Group, 165 Dufferin Street
Toronto, Ontario, Canada M6K 3H6

Distributed in Australia by Capricorn Link (Australia) Pty. Ltd.
P.O. Box 704, Windsor, NSW 2756 Australia

Manufactured in China

Sterling ISBN 13: 978-1-58816-655-5
ISBN 10: 1-58816-655-4

A warm toast.
Good company.
A fine wine.
May you enjoy all three.

. . .

Contents

· Toasts ·

Foreword

What would a wedding reception be without a toast from the best man? That all depends, of course, on what he says. If the speech is short, clever and in good taste, it will add enormously to the festivities. If, on the other hand, it drones on, is full of inside references or, worse, allusions to former girlfriends, it could cause embarrassment and will be forever remembered by the bride, not to mention her relatives.

When it comes to making a toast, knowing just what to say and exactly how to say it is an art that few have mastered. Hence, we offer a little help from *Town & Country*, whose authority in these matters dates back to 1846, when the magazine was born. The quotes gathered in this book have been uttered over centuries and for all sorts of occasions, weddings included. We hope one of these examples might come in handy or even inspire you to craft an original toast of your own.

As editor in chief of *Town & Country*, I attend more than my share of parties, dinners, corporate functions, cocktail receptions and holiday fetes. After listening to hundreds of toasts—and even having made a few myself—I have learned that giving a toast is not unlike making an acceptance speech. The less said, the better. Just be sure that every one of those few words count. How? By thinking in advance about what you want to say, by polishing your remarks so they sound smooth and, finally, by practicing. Just as a good comedian never ad libs, a good toastmaker doesn't wing it.

Now let me raise an imaginary glass and propose a toast to all of you who may one day be asked to stand up and have your say about someone who richly deserves recognition or about an important occasion worth noting. Then, by all means, let the party begin.

—PAMELA FIORI,
Editor in Chief, *Town & Country*

Introduction

You've been asked to mark a milestone in someone's life by proposing a toast and on paper, it seems as though it should be easy. After all, you know and like the guest (or guests) of honor and even feel that you have something meaningful to say. But when the time arrives, the strangest thing happens: you're at a loss for words and yet you can't stop talking. Like a best supporting starlet stumbling through her endless list of award-show thank-yous, a rambling toast is an awkward experience for everyone involved.

There are many reasons why mastering the art of making a toast is worth the time and trouble. First and most important, toasting is an age-old ritual that remains a vital part of honoring the special occasions in our lives, from the joyful celebration of birth or marriage to the sorrowful commemoration of a life that has passed. The practice of raising our glasses dates back to Biblical times, and the verb "toast" refers to the Roman custom of placing a piece of burnt bread in the communal wine goblet to absorb impurities and improve flavor, making the wine more palatable. The delicate clink of glasses that we now use to signal the end of a toast serves two purposes: it replicates the bell-like noise traditionally believed to "banish the devil," and since it is no longer the custom to drink from a communal goblet, this gesture is a way of emphasizing our shared experience.

Although the Irish—with their strong pub culture, long literary history, and love of poetry—are most famous for it, toasting is a multicultural practice, one that exists in every country from Eastern Europe to the Far East. Each culture may come with its own toasting etiquette, but no matter where we live, learning to rise to the occasion with well chosen words remains a way to express the feelings of common purpose created when we come together to observe a milestone. Offering a toast actually takes us beyond the role of witnesses; we become part of the ceremony.

One thing is for sure: the best toasts are short, personal, and tasteful. It helps to think of a toast as a compressed speech and employ the same structure when you begin to organize your thoughts: salutation (in which you greet the guest or guests of honor), statement of purpose (reiterate to the other guests the reason you are gathered together), and expression of point of view (or in this case, sentiment).

It is also important to match the right toast to the right occasion and some of the best examples can be taken from movies. In the legendary romantic triangle *Casablanca* (1942), Humphrey Bogart (as café owner Rick Blaine) delivers a minimal masterpiece that is full of longing when he toasts his lost love (played by Ingrid Bergman) by raising his glass and saying, "Here's looking at you, kid," and bachelor Hugh Grant makes a befuddled but charming toast in *Four Weddings and a Funeral* (1994) that starts off in a halting fashion but ends with the moving revelation that he is "constantly in awe of anyone who can make this kind of commitment."

Although both are testimonies to how expressive and effective the right toast can be, it helps to remember that there were screenwriters, directors, dialogue coaches, and who knows how many takes in order to get the timing and delivery just right. Giving a good toast—ideally one that is warm and charming and in-the-moment—is not something that comes naturally to most of us. "It usually takes more than three weeks to prepare a good impromptu speech," said Mark Twain, one of America's most beloved orators, and you might be surprised at how long it takes to master the art of appearing spontaneous.

Unless you have a room full of people at your disposal, it is hard to rehearse your toast under the same circumstances in which it will be offered. But once you know what you are going to say, you will be able to practice until the words come naturally to you (which in turn will help you pace your toast so that you are relaxed and not rushed during the real thing). Although it may not completely eliminate your nervousness on the big day, practicing can also provide the all-too-frequently missing piece of the public speaking puzzle—confidence.

WHERE TO BEGIN

It is a privilege to be asked to propose a toast, not a burden. If you cannot bring yourself to speak publicly, it is better to pass on the request by being completely candid: "As much as I'd love to participate, I just don't feel comfortable enough speaking in front of a group to be able to propose a toast." Instead, you might offer to express your sentiments and commemorate the celebration by writing a note to the honoree(s).

If you are doing the asking, do it well enough in advance so participants have time to compose and memorize their toasts. You may also set a time limit and suggest the tone you expect the toast to take.

The first step towards writing a good toast is to focus on your relationship to the guest (or guests) of honor and take stock of the emotion you want to express. Remember that there is a reason you were asked to give a toast and letting the other guests know the source of your connection to the honoree(s) makes a good introduction. This might mean opening your toast with something as straightforward as, "This marks the twentieth year that I have been lucky enough to call John my friend." Or explaining that, "I haven't known Susan for an unusually long time—just long enough to know that I can trust her to come through no matter what."

A toast should give voice to the way you feel and so, to best express yourself, use your own vocabulary. Even when you decide to draw your inspiration from a traditional toast or an emotionally significant quotation or poem, you don't have to repeat it word-for-word. You can use it as an inspirational framework, "translating" the words into language that is most natural to you. This simple step goes a long way towards keeping you relaxed and sounding sincere.

Take some ancient advice from the Greek playwright, Sophocles: "Much wisdom often goes with brevity of speech." In modern times, this means a toast that lasts anywhere from one to three minutes. Keeping it short means that you'll stay focused and guests will remain interested. It also means that you can memorize your speech and won't need to read from a cache of index cards, an act totally lacking in the personal touch. (Do we really believe award winners when they tell us that they never thought they'd be "up there," and then whip out a list of people to thank?)

The more informal the celebration (and the smaller the number of guests), the shorter and more direct your toast can be. There are times when proposing a toast can be a simple expression of a heartfelt sentiment, such as offering your thanks to the host and hostess for a wonderfully prepared meal, or wishing a friend a happy birthday with many more to come. However, more formal occasions (like a wedding or landmark anniversary) traditionally require more personalized toasts, often based on an anecdote about your relationship to the honoree(s).

No matter who howlingly funny you believe yourself to be, resist the temptation to walk that extremely fine line between telling tales and being tasteless. This is a toast, not a roast, an especially important distinction at weddings, when the guest list is sure to span several generations.

RISING TO THE OCCASION

Typically, a toast comes at a point in a celebration when there is a natural pause, for example, the window of opportunity that presents itself before or after the dessert course is served at a seated dinner. Take advantage of this lull to concentrate on the task at hand. If it is not possible for you to step away for a few moments in order to collect your thoughts, stay where you are and take a deep breath to center yourself.

There may or may not be a toastmaster who will introduce you. On formal occasions when there is a champagne toast (for example, a fiftieth wedding anniversary), the toastmaster is also responsible for coordinating the arrival of the filled glasses. At other times, people will toast with whatever beverage they are drinking.

In either situation, when it comes time for you to propose a toast, it is not necessary to clang on your glass with your fork (or anything else) to silence the room. You should be able to command attention by standing and saying in a loud, clear voice, "Good evening (morning, afternoon)," even though you might have to say it more than once. If that fails, you may ping your glass discreetly with a teaspoon to get attention (but a little goes a long way).

Face the honoree(s); smile; offer your toast.

Focus yourself (and the guests) by stating why you are gathered together and, when the occasion calls for it, why you were asked to give a toast: "We're here today to celebrate the fiftieth anniversary of my dear aunt and uncle, Bob and Judy Woodson." This is the perfect launching pad to share an anecdote about your relationship.

When you are finished speaking, punctuate the end of your toast by asking guests to raise their glasses (done by extending the arm straight out from the shoulder, not over your head like a flag) and drinking to the honoree (s). It is customary to delicately tap glasses with the people closest to you; it is not necessary to stretch across the table in order to accommodate those outside arm's reach. All that's required is a nod and a smile.

If the toast is being offered in your honor, do not drink. Wait until everyone takes a ceremonial sip, and then stand to offer your thanks . . . briefly.

WEDDING TOASTS

Wedding toasts are the most structured and generally follow a set protocol which should be established in advance. Depending on the size of the wedding party and the presence of one or both sets of parents as well as other family members, there can be quite a list of people who will be asked to speak.

If you are hosting a large wedding celebration, keeping the toasting list to a minimum can mean asking those outside the bridal couple's most intimate circle to propose their toast at the rehearsal dinner or wedding breakfast.

If you have been chosen to offer a wedding toast, stay within the boundaries of your role. For example, if you have been given the honor of acting as a best man, your job is not to welcome family and friends to the wedding. This is traditionally the role of the father of the bride—he is the "giver" (and often the payer)—or the groom himself. Instead, as the man who knows the groom best, confidently offer your congratulations with the intimacy of someone who has stood by through other milestones in his life and borne witness to his growing love and betrothal. (Intimate and embarrassing are not the same thing.)

The groom's speech is made on behalf of the couple and primarily acts as a public expression of gratitude to the family and friends who have attended, singling out their parents and those in the wedding party.

Although it is not a common practice, there are times when the bride may also offer a toast. Her speech should not just duplicate the sentiments of the groom, but express her own happiness with her new husband and family.

What follows is a *Town & Country* collection of toasts and appropriate quotations that range from traditional to international. Some are literary; some folk wisdom.

Many can stand alone; others can be used to inspire your own writing. But no matter when and where and to whom you are offering a toast, remember that eloquence is admirable, but being able to express heartfelt emotion is enviable. Guests will remember a good toast (and may even repeat it for years to come), and we offer these simple guidelines as a way to help you make it memorable for everyone.

—FRANCINE MAROUKIAN

Toasts

America

To the United States, where each man is
protected by the Constitution
regardless of whether he has ever taken the
time to read it.

Here's to the Army and Navy,
And the battles they have won.
Here's to America's colors—
The colors that never run.

Here's to the land we love and
the love of the land.

To the land we live in, love, and would die for.

To our flag—may its stars light the way
And its stripes guide our steps in the
everlasting cause of peace.

Our country, our whole country,
and nothing but our country!
—DANIEL WEBSTER

To America—half-brother of all the world!

To America—
"With all its faults and blemishes, this country
gives a man elbowroom to do what
is nearest his heart."
—ERIC HOFFER, **FIRST THINGS, LAST THINGS**

Historic Toasts

What follows is a sampling of special toasts that were tied to a specific cause, place or event in history.

Here's to the squire who goes on parade,
Here's to the citizen soldier.
Here's to the merchant
who fights for his trade,
Whom danger increasingly
makes bolder,
Let mirth appear,
Every heart cheer,
The toast that I give is to
the brave volunteer.

—AMERICAN REVOLUTION

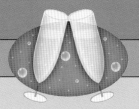

Freedom from mobs as well as kings.
—AMERICAN, LATE EIGHTEENTH CENTURY

Ladies and Gentlemen, this is the last time I shall drink to your health as a public man. I do it with all sincerity, wishing you all possible happiness.
—GEORGE WASHINGTON GAVE THIS TOAST ON MARCH 3, 1797, THE DAY BEFORE HE RETIRED FROM OFFICE, AT A DINNER HE HELD FOR PRESIDENT-ELECT JOHN ADAMS.

Ask nothing that is not clearly right, and submit to nothing that is wrong.
—ANDREW JACKSON'S MOTTO, OFTEN USED AS A TOAST IN THE NINETEENTH CENTURY

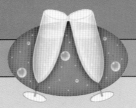

To the total abolition of the slave trade.

—ABOLITIONIST'S TOAST

A mighty nation mourns thee yet;
Thy gallant crew—their awful fate;
And justice points her straight,
Lest we forget—lest we forget!

—ON THE SINKING OF THE **MAINE**

May it always carry messages
of happiness.

—ON THE CHRISTENING OF THE HONOLULU
CABLE BETWEEN SAN FRANCISCO AND HAWAII,
DECEMBER 15, 1902.

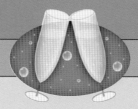

Gentlemen, I believe your victories
were won on water.

—WILLIAM JENNINGS BRYAN.
ASKED TO TOAST THE BRITISH NAVY,
HE DID SO WITH A GLASS OF WATER.

Here's to my car and your car,
and may they never meet.

—FROM THE EARLY DAYS OF THE AUTOMOBILE

Here's to today!
For tomorrow we may be radioactive.

—EARLY ATOMIC AGE TOAST

. . .

To America: her lovely women
and her brave men.

America, my country, great and free,
Heart of the world, I drink to thee.

One flag, one land, one heart,
One nation evermore.

—OLIVER WENDELL HOLMES

.   .   .

Anniversary

To you on your anniversary,
May every new day bring more happiness
than yesterday.

May you grow old on one pillow.
—ARMENIAN TOAST

Here's to you both—
a beautiful pair,
on the birthday
of your love affair.

Here is to loving, to romance, to us.
May we travel together through time.
We alone count as none,
but together we're one,
For our partnership puts love to rhyme.
—IRISH

Let anniversaries come and
let anniversaries go—but may your happiness
continue on forever.

To your coming anniversaries—may they be
outnumbered only by your coming pleasures.

We've holidays and holy days,
and memory days galore;
And when we've toasted every one,
I offer just one more.
So let us lift our glasses high,
and drink a silent toast—
The day, deep buried in each heart,
that each one loves the most.

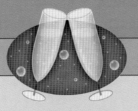

A Vintage Toast

To Longevity

May we love as long as we live,
and live as long as we may love.

. . .

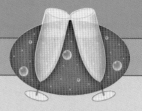

A Vintage Toast

To a Cool Head

Drink to the man who keeps his head,
though he loses his heart.

. . .

With fifty years between you
And your well-kept wedding vow,
The Golden Age, old friends of mine,
Is not a fable now.

—THE GOLDEN WEDDING AT LONGWOOD,
BY JOHN GREENLEAF WHITTIER

To my spouse,
Because I love you truly,
Because you love me, too,
My very greatest happiness,
Is sharing life with you.

. . .

Birthday

May you have been born on your lucky star
and may that star never lose its twinkle.

May you live to be a hundred years with
one extra year to repent.

—IRISH

It is not the years in your life,
But the life in your years that counts.

—ADLAI STEVENSON

Time marches on!
Now tell the truth—
Where did you find
The fountain of youth?

To our favorite old hippie.
Let me assure you that this is a real
celebration and not an acid flashback.

To the old, long life and treasure;
To the young, all health and pleasure.

—BEN JONSON

To our friend who is aging wonderfully.
Nothing about you is old,
except a few of your jokes.

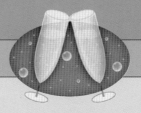

Jewish Toasts

The primary Jewish toast is the Hebrew *L'chayim*, which means "to life," or "to your health." *Mazel tov* is also used as a toast. Leo Rosten, in his *Joys of Yiddish*, explains when to use them: "Some innocents confuse *L'chayim* with *mazel tov*, using one when the other would be appropriate. There is no reason to err. *L'chayim* is used whenever one would say 'Your health,' 'Cheers!' or (I shudder to say) 'Here's mud in your eye.' *Mazel tov!* is used as 'congratulations.'"

· · ·

Here's to a man who's discovered what really separates the men from the boys—many years.

To age. In the words of Frank Lloyd Wright, "The longer I live, the more beautiful life becomes."

May you live to be a hundred—and decide the rest for yourself.

To old age, may it always be ten years older than I am.

May we live to learn well, and learn to live well.

To the most closely guarded secret in this country—your real age.

May you live as long as you want, may you never want as long as you live.

To your birthday, glass held high,
Glad it's you that's older—not I.

The good die young—here's hoping that you
may live to a ripe old age.

You're not as young as you used to be,
But you're not as old as you're going to be,
So watch it!

—IRISH

To wish you joy on your birthday
And all the whole year through,
For all the best that life can hold
Is none too good for you.

To a healthy year,
And many of them.

Although another year is past
You look no older than
the last!

God grant you many and happy years,
Till, when the last has crowned you,
The dawn of endless days appears,
And heaven is shining round you!
—OLIVER WENDELL HOLMES

Happy birthday to you
And many to be
With friends that are true
As you are to me!

Long life to you and may you die
in your own bed.

May the good Lord take a liking to you,
But not too soon!

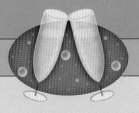

A Vintage Toast

To Time

May he permit us all to write
our own epitaphs.

. . .

A Vintage Toast

To Harder Times

May we keep a little of the fuel of youth
to warm our body in old age.

. . .

Another candle on your cake?
Well, that's no cause to pout,
Be glad that you have strength enough
To blow the damn thing out.

Another year older? Think this way:
Just one day older than yesterday!

Do not resist growing old—many are denied
the privilege.

Here's to you on your birthday,
It's better to be over the hill than under it!

Here's a health to the future;
A sigh for the past;
We can love and remember,
And hope to last,
And for all the base lies
That the almanacs hold,
While there's love in the heart
We can never grow old.

To middle age, when we begin to exchange
our emotions for symptoms.

A health, and many of them. Birthdays were
never like this when I had 'em.

Many happy returns of the day of your birth;
Many blessings to brighten your
pathway on earth;
Many friendships to cheer and
provoke you to mirth;
Many feastings and frolics to
add to your girth.

—ROBERT H. LORD

.   .   .

Children

A new life begun,
Like father, like son.

—IRISH

Like one, like the other,
Like daughter, like mother.

—IRISH

Here's to one who born will be,
Born of the body, sowed of the soul,
Born of the flesh of you and me.

Here is the toast of the moon and the stars,
To the child . . . who will soon be ours.

A lovely being scarcely formed or molded,
A rose with all its sweetest leaves yet folded.

—LORD BYRON

To the new baby, who,
As the parents will soon find out,
Is the perfect example of minority rule.

Here's to the baby—man to be—
May he be as fine as thee!
Here's to baby—woman to be—
May she be as sweet as thee!

May there be a generation of children
On the children of your children.

—IRISH

Here's to the stork,
A most valuable bird,
That inhabits the residence districts.
He doesn't sing tunes,
Nor yield any plumes,
But he helps the vital statistics.

May he/she grow twice as tall as yourself
and half as wise.

—IRISH

Here's to adolescence, that period
When children feel their parents
Should be told the facts of life.

Here's to children,
The truest legacy we leave the world.

To our grandchildren,
Our revenge on our children!

—IRISH

Christmas

Here's to the day of good will,
cold weather, and warm hearts.

Here's to the merriest of Christmases!

A Christmas wish—
May you never forget
what is worth remembering
or remember
what is best forgotten.

—IRISH

To full stomachs and merry hearts.

I wish you a Merry Christmas
And a Happy New Year,
A pocket full of money
And a cellar full of beer!

May the Virgin and her Child lift your latch
on Christmas night.

—IRISH

*(This refers to the old Irish custom of leaving the door unbolted and
a candle in the window for Mary on her way to Bethlehem.)*

May you be as contended as Christmas finds
you all the year round.

—IRISH

May you live as long as you Wish,
and have all you Wish as long as you live.
This is my Christmas Wish for you.

—IRISH

Then let us be merry and taste the good cheer,
And remember old Christmas comes
but once a year.

May you never be without a drop at Christmas.

—IRISH

Here's to the holly with its bright red berry.
Here's to Christmas, let's make it merry.

Here's to us all!
God bless us every one!

—TINY TIM'S TOAST, FROM **A CHRISTMAS CAROL**,
BY CHARLES DICKENS

Peace and plenty for many
a Christmas to come.

—IRISH

Here's wishing you more happiness
Than words can ever tell,
Not just alone for Christmas
But for all the year as well.

Holly and ivy hanging up
And something wet in every cup.

—IRISH

At Christmas play and make good cheer
For Christmas comes but once a year.

—THOMAS TUSSER

May peace and plenty be the first
To lift the latch on your door,
And happiness be guided to your home
By the candle of Christmas.

—IRISH

.   .   .

Fathers

To my father. If I can become half the man
he is, I'll have achieved greatness.

To Father. May the love and respect
we express toward him
make up, at least in part, for the worry and
care we have visited upon him.

To Dad:
Even though you never get our names right,
we know you love us.

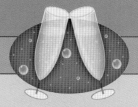

A Vintage Toast

To the memory of George Washington,
the childless father of seventy millions.

—POPULAR NINETEENTH-CENTURY TOAST

· · ·

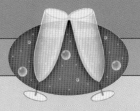

A Vintage Toast

*A toast by made by
the hopeful heir:*

Here's health to those I love,
and wealth to those who love me.

. . .

My father has given me the greatest
treasure a father can give,
A piece of himself.

.   .   .

Fishing

Here's to Fishing—a grand delusion
enthusiastically promoted by glorious liars in
old clothes.

—DON MARQUIS

To the fish—a creature that goes on vacation at
about the same time most fishermen do.

Here's to the fish that I may catch;
So large that even I,
When talking of it afterward,
Will never need to lie.

Here's to our fisherman bold;
Here's to the fish he caught;
Here's to the one that got away;
Here's to the one he bought.

May the holes in your net be
no bigger than your fish.

—IRISH

Rod and line: May they never part company.

Here's to the steady fisherman,
Who never reels home!

To fishing—if it interferes with business,
Give up the business.

To the fish who may come and go, but the
memory of afternoons on the stream endures.

Here's to the one that got away!

A Vintage Toast

To the Pessimist

Malediction upon the man who
will not see the light.

. . .

We fall for his tales,
Hook, line, and sinker;
He doesn't catch much,
But he's a great thinker.

To sending flies flying and starting fish frying.

Here's to the folks who know that old fishers
never die—they just smell that way.

Here's to our favorite fisherman:
May he live to see his stories come true.

May good things come to those who bait.

Fishing is the chance to wash one's soul with
pure air. It brings meekness and inspiration,
reduces our egotism, soothes our troubles and
shames our wickedness.

—HERBERT HOOVER

A bad day of fishing
is still better than a good day at work.
—BUMPER STICKER

Here's to the noble sport of fishing,
A hobby that we're all hooked on!

. . .

Food

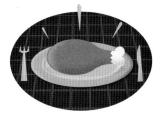

Eat, drink and be merry
for tomorrow you diet.

Let the dogs wait a long time.
—IRISH WISH FOR A LENGTHY AND AMPLE DINNER

To Mom's cooking:
May my wife never find out how bad
it really was.

To soup:
May it be seen and not heard.

Good pies and strong beer.
—FROM **POOR ROBIN'S ALMANACK**, 1695

Eat thy bread with joy,
and drink thy wine with a merry heart.
—ECCLESIASTES 9:7

. . .

Fourth of July

To our country! Lift your glasses!
To its sun-capped mountain passes,
To its forest, to its streams,
To its memories, its dreams,
To its laughter, to its tears,
To the hope that after-years
Find us plodding on the way
Without so much tax to pay.

Here's to our native land!
May we live for it and die in it.

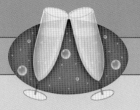

A Vintage Toast

To Our Army

Here's to Uncle Sam's fighters,
Models of all that is brave,
Terrors to all who're unfair.

. . .

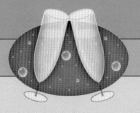

A Vintage Toast

To Our Navy

From its dandy Admiral to
the man behind the gun.

· · ·

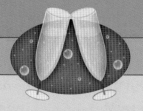

A Vintage Toast

To the President

God save the President
of the United States,
and he'll save God's country.

. . .

Our Country:
To her we drink, for her we pray,
Our voices silent never;
For her we'll fight, come what may,
The stars and stripes forever!

—STEPHEN DECATUR

Here's to the memory
Of the man
That raised the corn
That fed the goose
That bore the quill
That made the pen
That wrote the Declaration of Independence.

Here's to the memory of those
who died for freedom.

•   •   •

Friendship

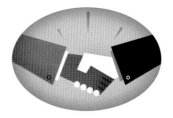

Absent friends—though out of sight we
recognize them with our glasses.

Here's to us that are here,
to you that are there,
And the rest of us everywhere.

—RUDYARD KIPLING

A friend may well be reckoned the
masterpiece of Nature.

—RALPH WALDO EMERSON

Lest auld acquaintance be forgot
And fail to come to mind,
A cup of kindness on the spot,
Let's drain for Auld Lang Syne.

—ROBERT BURNS

There is no possession more valuable than
a true and faithful friend.

—SOCRATES

May friendship propose the toast, and
sincerity drink it.

A health to you,
A wealth to you,
And the best that life can give you.

Here's to _____, equal to none.

A day for toil, an hour for sport,
But for a friend life is too short.

—RALPH WALDO EMERSON

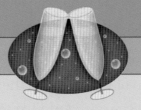

A Vintage Toast

To Discussion

Let this toast pass 'round.
In discussion, not concussion,
Is true joy found.

. . .

Here's to one sweetheart,
one bottle and one friend,
The first beautiful, the second full,
and the last forever faithful.

May fortune still be kind to you,
And happiness be true to you,
And life be long and good to you,
Is the toast of all your friends to you.

May we have a few real friends rather than a
thousand acquaintances.

To friends: As long as we are able
To lift our glass from the table.

Here's to a friendship that has always been
filled with laughter.

My heart is as full as my glass when
I drink to you, old friend.

A Vintage Toast

To the Sixth Sense

May the right person say the right thing
to the right person in the right way at the
right time and in the right place.

. . .

A Vintage Toast

To Everybody

To you, and yours, and theirs, and mine,
I pledge with you, their health and wine.

. . .

May the friends of our youth be
the companions of our old age.

May we never want for a friend,
nor a glass to give him.

Here's to you, as good as you are,
And here's to me, as bad as I am;
As bad as I am, as good as you are,
I'm as good as you are as bad as I am.
—OLD SCOTTISH TOAST

Here's to those of us who are friends—
And let the rest of the world make its own
arrangements.

Friendship: May differences of opinion
cement it.

Here's to friendship,
One soul in two bodies!

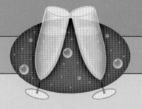

A Vintage Toast

To Staunchness

To honest opinion—right or wrong—
here's to honest opinion.

. . .

Here's to you and here's to me,
Wherever we may roam;
And here's to the health and happiness
Of the ones who are left at home.

Bread to our friendship,
Salt to keep it true,
Water is for a welcome,
And wine to drink with you.
—FRENCH PROVERB

Friendship is the wine of life.
Let's drink of it and to it.

Here's all that's fine to you!
Books and old wine to you!
Girls be divine to you!
—RICHARD HOVEY

Here's to a friend. He knows you well
and likes you just the same.

A Vintage Toast

To Loyalty

Before it may invective and persuasion
lay down their arms.

. . .

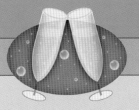

A Vintage Toast

To Money

To money—a friend in need,
and a need indeed.

. . .

Here's to a cold night, warm friends,
and a good drink to give them.

Here's to our friendship;
May it be reckoned
Long as a lifetime,
Close as a second.

Here's to Eternity—may we spend it in as good
company as this night finds us.

Here's to our friends . . . and the strength
to put up with them!

—ADVERTISEMENT FOR THE MOVIE
THE FOUR SEASONS

Pour deep the rosy wine and drink
a toast with me;
Here's to three: Thee, Wine,
and Camaraderie!

—TOM MOORE

Here's to the four hinges of Friendship—
Swearing, Lying, Stealing, and Drinking.
When you swear, swear by your country;
When you lie, lie for a pretty woman;
When you steal, steal away from bad company;
And when you drink, drink with me.

Love to one, friendship to many,
and good will to all.

Old friends are scarce,
New friends are few;
Here's hoping I've found
One of each in you.

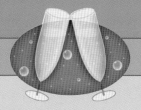

A Vintage Toast

To Our Secrets

May they never be imparted to a
stranger, for they are scarcely safe
with a friend.

. . .

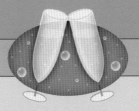

A Vintage Toast

To Laughter

The bright coinage of
the bank of good will.

. . .

Here's to you, old friend,
may you live a thousand years,
Just to sort of cheer things in this vale of
human tears;
And may I live a thousand too—a thousand—
less a day.
'Cause I wouldn't care to be on earth and hear
you'd passed away.

Here's to our faraway friends,
May their spirits be with us,
As soon as these spirits are in us.

The Lord gives our relatives,
Thank God we can choose our friends.

The world is gay and colorful,
And life itself is new.
And I am very grateful for
The friend I found in you.

To my friend. If we ever disagree,
may you be in the right.

To our best friends, who know the worst about
us but refuse to believe it.

Here's to absent friends,
And here's twice to absent enemies.

—IRISH

We'll think of all the friends we know
And drink to all worth drinking to.

Merry met and merry part,
I drink to thee with all my heart.

May your tobacco never run out,
Your library never turn musty,
Your cellar never go dry,
And your friends never turn foes.

Good friends, good food, good times!

·   ·   ·

Graduates

A toast to the graduate—in a class by him/herself.

May hope whisper in their ears sweet promises that kind fortune will quickly ratify.

Here's to optimism, where every obstacle Is but a stepping-stone to your success.

May you live a goodly number of years, and upon each one carve the word "success."

All that Adam had, all that Caesar could,
you have and can do. . . . Build, therefore,
your own world.

—RALPH WALDO EMERSON

Here's to your future, the best way to predict it
Is to create it!

May you have the best life has to offer.

. . .

Guests

Here's to our guest—
Don't let him rest.
But keep his elbow bending.
'Tis time to drink—
Full time to think
Tomorrow—when you're mending.

We've had toasts to our hosts, now one to our
guests, without whom it wouldn't be much
of a party.

All our guests make us happy,
Some by coming and others by going.

Here's a toast to all who are here,
No matter where you're from;
May the best day you have seen
Be worse than your worst to come.

Our house is ever at your service.

See, your guests approach;
Address yourself to entertain them sprightly,
And let's be red with mirth.

—WILLIAM SHAKESPEARE

The ornament of a house is the guests
who frequent it.

A Vintage Toast

To Tonight

Though tomorrow, friends,
will be another day,
tomorrow night some may be far away.

. . .

A Vintage Toast

To Conviviality

May its harmonies send discord
howling on her way.

. . .

To Our Guest! A friend of our friend is doubly our friend. Here's to him.

Happy is the house that shelters a friend.

—RALPH WALDO EMERSON

.   .   .

Happiness

I wish you all the joy you can wish.

—WILLIAM SHAKESPEARE

Happiness is like a kiss,
It feels better when you give it to
someone else.

Here's a toast to happiness,
It sneaks in through a door you didn't know
you left open.

—JOHN BARRYMORE

To each, to all, happiness, health,
and fortunes grown tall.

May we breakfast with Health, dine with
Friendship, crack a bottle with Mirth, and sup
with the goddess Contentment.

Here's to living well,
'Tis the best revenge.

May we be happy and our enemies know it.

Here's to happy times,
May they come often and stay long!

I raise my glass to wish you
your heart's desire!

—RUSSIAN

May you be merry and lack nothing.

—WILLIAM SHAKESPEARE

Health

Here's to your health! You make Age curious,
Time furious, and all of us envious.

To our health. May it remain with us
long after we die.

Early to rise and early to bed
makes a male healthy and wealthy
and dead.

—JAMES THURBER

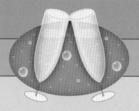

Around the World

French: *À votre santé!* (To your health!)

German: *Prost!* (Cheers!)

Hebrew: *L'chayim!* (To life!)

Italian: *Salute!* (Health!)
or *Cin cin!* (Cheers!)

Japanese: *Kanpai!* (Cheers!)

Portuguese: *Saúde!* (Health!)

Spanish: *¡Salud!* (Health!)

Swedish: *Skål!* (Health!)

. . .

Here's a health to everyone;
Peace on earth, and heaven won.

Here's to your health—
a long life and an easy death to you.

The health of the salmon to you: a long life,
a full heart, and a wet mouth!

. . .

Host and Hostess

To our host: An excellent man; for, is not a
man fairly judged by the company he keeps?

I thank you for your welcome
which was cordial,
And your cordial, which is welcome.

Let's drink to the maker of the feast,
our friend and host.
May his generous heart, like his good wine,
only grow mellower with the years.

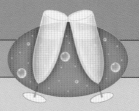

A Vintage Toast

To a Nightcap

Brew me a cup for a winter's night,
For the wind howls loud,
and the furies fight;
Spice it with love and stir it with care,
And I'll toast your bright eyes,
My sweetheart fair.

. . .

May the roof above us never fall in, and may
we friends gathered below never fall out.

May you be Hung, Drawn, and Quartered!
Yes—Hung with diamonds,
Drawn in a coach and four,
And quartered in the best houses in the land.

Good company, good wine, good welcome
make good people.

—WILLIAM SHAKESPEARE

To the sun that warmed the vineyard,
To the juice that turned to wine,
To the host that cracked the bottle,
And made it yours and mine.

To our hostess! She's a gem.
We love her, God bless her.
And the devil take her husband.

To our host: The rapturous, wild, and ineffable
pleasure of drinking at somebody
else's expense.

—HENRY SAMBROOKE LEIGH, 1870

What's a table richly spread
Without a woman at its head?

A toast to our hosts
From all of us,
May they soon be the guests
Of each and every one of us!

Here's to our hostess, considerate and sweet;
Her wit is endless, but when do we eat?

I drink to the general joy of the whole table.

—WILLIAM SHAKESPEARE

Nothing but the best for our hostess,
That's why she has us as friends.

It is around the table that friends understand
best the warmth of being together.

—ITALIAN SAYING

. . .

Husbands

Here's to the first man who could win both
   my heart and my mother's approval.

May your life be long and sunny
And your husband fat and funny.

Here's to that most provoking man,
The man of wisdom deep,
Who never talks when he takes his rest,
But only smiles in his sleep.

Irish

May the face of every good news
And the back of every bad news
Be towards us.

—IRISH

A goose in your garden except on
Christmas day.

And may you be half-an-hour in heaven
Before the devil knows you're dead.
Slante!

[Pronounced *slawn-cheh*; it means Health!]

May you have warm words on a cold evening,
A full moon on a dark night,
And the road downhill all the way to your door.

Here's a health to your enemies' enemies!

Here's to eyes in your head and
none in your spuds!

May bad fortune follow you all your days,
And never catch up!

May the saints protect you,
And sorrow neglect you,
And bad luck to the one
That doesn't respect you.

Here's to health, peace, and prosperity;
May the flower of love never be nipped by the
frost of disappointment; nor shadow of grief
fall among a member of this circle.

Here's to the land of the shamrock so green,
Here's to each lad and his darling colleen,
Here's to the ones we love dearest and most,
And may God save old Ireland—that's an
Irishman's toast.

Here's to your health
May God bring you luck
And may your journey be smooth and happy.

May the path of hell grow green
For lack of travelers.

May you get all your wishes but one,
So you always have something to strive for.

Here's that we may always have
A clean shirt
A clean conscience
And a guinea in our pocket.

May the road rise to meet you.
May the wind be always at your back,
the sun shine warm upon your face,
the rain fall soft upon your fields,
and until we meet again
may God hold you in the hollow of His hand.

May you have food and raiment,
A soft pillow for your head,
May you be forty years in heaven
Before the devil knows you're dead!

When money's tight and hard to get,
And your horse is an also-ran,
When all you have is a heap of debt
A pint of plain is your only man.

May I see you grey
And combing your children's hair.

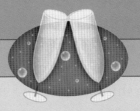

A Vintage Toast

To the Novelist

Unlimited editions.

. . .

May the sun shine warm upon your face
and the rains fall soft upon your fields.
May there always be work for your hands to do.
May your purse always hold a coin or two.
May the sun always shine on your windowpane.
May a rainbow be certain to follow each rain.
May the hand of a friend always be near you.
May God fill your heart with gladness
to cheer you.

May we all be alive this time in twelve months.

May leprechauns dance over your bed,
And bring you sweet dreams.

May you have the hindsight to know where
you've been, the foresight to know where
you're going, and the insight to know when
you're going too far.

May you look back on the past with as much pleasure as you look forward to the future.

May your fire never go out.

To your very good health,
May you live to be as old as your jokes.

May your well never run dry.

To warm words on a cold day.

Health and long life to you
The woman of your choice to you
A child every year to you
Land without rent to you
And may you die in Ireland.

Your Health! May we have one together in ten years time and a few in between.

May the strength of three be in your journey.

May the rocks in your field all turn to gold.

Here's to you and yours and to mine and ours,
And if mine and ours ever come
across you and yours,
I hope you and yours will do as much
for mine and ours,
As mine and ours have done
for you and yours!

. . .

Libations

Drink and be merry, for our time on earth is
short, and death lasts forever.

To champagne,
the drink that makes you see double,
And feel single!

When I read about the evils of drinking,
I gave up reading.

—HENNY YOUNGMAN

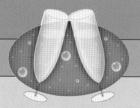

A Vintage Toast

To Bohemia

Where the sorrows of the morning are
forgotten in the joys of the night.

. . .

Drink today and drown all sorrow.
You shall perhaps not do't tomorrow.
Best while you have it, use your breath;
There is no drinking after death.

—FRANCIS BEAMONT AND JOHN FLETCHER,
THE BLOOD BROTHER

Drink with impunity—
Or anyone who happens to invite you!

—ARTEMUS WARD

Lift 'em high and drain 'em dry,
To the guy who says, "My turn to buy!"

Here's to temperance—in moderation!

Here's to a long life and a merry one,
A quick death and an easy one,
A pretty girl and a true one,
A cold bottle and another one.

I'm tired of drinking toasts
For each small glass of gin.
Let's toss out all the hooey
And toss the liquor in.

Let us have wine and women,
mirth and laughter
Sermons and soda water the day after.

—LORD BYRON

One bottle for four of us!
Thank God there's no more of us!

If all be true that I do think,
There are *Five Reasons* we should drink;
Good Wine, a Friend, or being Dry,
Or lest should be by and by;
Or any other Reason why.

—HENRY ALDRICH

Too much work, and no vacation,
Deserves at least a small libation.
So hail! my friends, and raise your glasses;
Work's the curse of the drinking classes.

What would you like to drink to?
To about three in the morning.

In heaven there is no beer,
So we'd better drink it here!

Here's to the man who takes the pledge,
Who keeps his word and does not hedge,
Who won't give up and won't give in
Till the last man's out and there's no more gin.

Drink! for you know not whence you come,
nor why;
Drink! for you know not why you go,
nor where.

—FROM THE **RUBAIYAT OF OMAR KHAYYAM**

Gentlemen, start your livers!

Drink and be merry, for our time on earth is
short, and death lasts forever.

—AMPHIS

Here's to you,
And here's to me;
But as you're not here,
Here's two to me.

Here's to champagne, the drink divine,
That makes us forget our troubles;
It's made of a dollar's worth of wine
And four dollars worth of bubbles.

I drink to your health when I'm with you,
I drink to your health when I'm alone,
I drink to your health so often
I'm beginning to worry about my own.

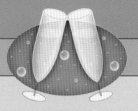

A Vintage Toast

To Mornings After

Here's to the good time I must have had!

. . .

To the cocktail party where olives are speared
and friends stabbed.

Here's to the ten stages of drunkenness:
1. witty and charming
2. rich and famous
3. benevolent
4. clairvoyant
5. screw dinner
6. patriotic
7. crank up the Enola Gay
8. witty and charming, part II
9. invisible, and lastly
10. bulletproof

Candy is dandy,
But liquor is quicker.

—OGDEN NASH

• • •

Life

May we always sail in pleasure's boat.

Be glad of life!
Because it gives you the chance
to love and work,
To play and to look up at the stars.

—HENRY VAN DYKE

Here's to beauty, wit, and wine, and to a full
stomach, a full purse, and a light heart.

May we live respected and die regretted.

May the clouds in your life form only a
background for a lovely sunset.

All that gives you pleasure.

It is best to rise from life as from the banquet,
neither thirsty nor drunken.

—ARISTOTLE

I wish thee health,
I wish thee wealth,
I wish thee gold in store,
I wish thee heaven upon earth—
What could I wish thee more?

I drink to the days that are.

—WILLIAM MORRIS

To Life. The first half is ruined by our parents and the second half by our children.

So live that when you come to die, even the undertaker will feel sorry for you.

——MARK TWAIN

· · ·

Love

Love doesn't make the world go 'round.
Love is what makes the ride worthwhile.

—FRANKLIN P. JONES

Because I love you truly,
Because you love me, too,
My very greatest happiness
Is sharing life with you.

'Twas not into my ear you whispered,
but into my heart.

—JUDY GARLAND

Do you love me
Or do you not?
You told me once
But I forgot.

Here's to Love—the only fire against which
there is no insurance.

I have known many,
Liked a few,
Loved one –
Here's to you!

Here's to fertility—the toast of agriculture
and the bane of love.

Here's to love and unity,
Dark corners and opportunity.

Here's looking at you, kid.
—HUMPHREY BOGART IN **CASABLANCA**

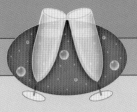

A Vintage Toast

To Eros

To the garden of Eros—may we gather there, no poisoned flower.

. . .

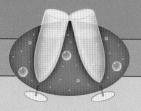

A Vintage Toast

To Lovers

The have-beens,
the are-nows,
and the may-bes.

. . .

Here's to one and only one,
And may that one be he
Who loves but one and only one,
And may that one be me.

Love cometh like sunshine after the rain.

—WILLIAM SHAKESPEARE

Here's to the pictures on my desk.
May they never meet.

Here's to the wings of love—
May they never moult a feather;
Till my big boots and your little shoes
Are under the bed together.

Love is the greatest refreshment in life.

—PABLO PICASSO

Where love is concerned,
Too much is never enough.

To us, we may not have it all together,
But together we have it all!

Here's to the woman that I love
And here's to the woman that loves me,
And here's to all those that love her that I love,
And to those that love her that love me.

Here's to this water,
Wishing it were wine,
Here's to you, my darling,
Wishing you were mine.

Here's to you,
May you live as long as you want to,
May you want to as long as you live.

To my Valentine,
I love you not only for what you are,
But what I am when I am with you.

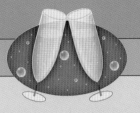

A Vintage Toast

To Our Sweethearts

Our sweethearts;
may they ever seem as sweet,
and ours always be their hearts.

. . .

Here's to you who halves my sorrows and
doubles my joys.

I love you more than yesterday,
less than tomorrow.

I would be friends with you
and have your love.

Let's drink to love,
Which is nothing—
Unless it's divided by two.

If love makes the world go round,
then you make it spin.

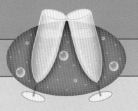

A Vintage Toast

To Virtue

That is to say—Discretion.

.   .   .

Wine comes in at the mouth,
And love comes in at the eye,
That's all we shall know for truth,
Before we grow old and die.
I lift the glass to my mouth,
I look at you, and I sigh.

—W. B. YEATS, **A DRINKING SONG**

. . .

Luck

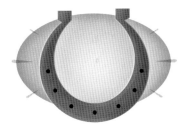

As you slide down the banister of life
May the splinters never face the wrong way.

Then welcome, stranger, cheer be thine,
If though art a friend, or a friend of mine,
Here's luck . . .

—JAMES MONROE McLEAN, **THE BOOK OF WINE**

May the luck of the Irish possess you,
May the devil fly off with your worries,
And may God bless you forever and ever!

—IRISH

A Vintage Toast

To the Good Thing

When it's exclusively our own.

. . .

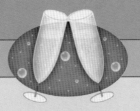

A Vintage Toast

To Moral Strength

May we cultivate it, particularly,
to withstand the fascinations of
the great god, chance.

. . .

To my friend—luck 'til the end!

May Dame Fortune ever smile on you,
But never her daughter, Miss Fortune.

When going up the hill of Prosperity,
May you never meet a friend coming down.

Here's to prosperity. . .
and the wisdom to use it well.

May your blessings outnumber
The shamrocks that grow,
And may trouble avoid you
Wherever you go.

—IRISH

.   .   .

Marriage

Here's to marriage, the high sea for which no compass has yet been invented!

—HEINRICH HEINE

Marriage is a wonderful institution, but who wants to live in an institution?

—GROUCHO MARX

Marriages are all happy,
It's having breakfast together that causes all the trouble!

A Vintage Toast

To Matrimony

Gentlemen, may you never scold a wife,
nor wive a scold.

. . .

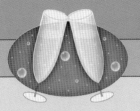

A Vintage Toast

To the Homely Three

A good book,
a bright light,
and an easy chair.

. . .

The greatest of all arts is the art
of living together.

To get the full value of joy, you must have
someone to divide it with.

—MARK TWAIN

Here's to marriage, which is a lot like the army,
Everyone complains, but you'd be surprised
By the large number that reenlist!

—JAMES GARNER

Keep your marriage brimming,
With love from the loving cup,
Whenever you're wrong, admit it,
Whenever you're right, shut up!

—OGDEN NASH

May your marriage be like a mighty ship,
Always holding a true and steady course,
Weathering rough seas with strength
and courage,
And sailing calm waters with style and grace.

.　.　.

Men

To the men I've loved,
To the men I've kissed,
My heartfelt apologies
To the men I've missed!

Here's to the man whose best girl is his
mother, and whose sweetheart is his wife.

To man, give him an inch
And he thinks he's a ruler!

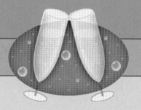

A Vintage Toast

To Baldness

To our bald friend,
whose head is a shining example!

. . .

A Vintage Toast

To the Cad

Malediction upon the man who has
more tongue than discretion.

. . .

Mothers

Here's to Mother—may the love and
appreciation of these later days overshadow
the worries we caused her in our childhood.

Here's to the noblest woman
that God ever made
He never made one such another
Here's to my Mother!

To our fathers' sweethearts,
Our mothers!

Here's to the happiest hours of my life—
Spent in the arms of another man's wife;
My mother!

To Mother—may she live long enough to forget
what fiends we used to be.

You may have a friend,
you may have a lover,
but don't forget,
your best friend is your mother.
—TRADITIONAL AUTOGRAPH ALBUM INSCRIPTION

To Mother:
The one who loves when fortune's bright,
But more when the sky's o'er-cast;
Whose heart reveals, yet more conceals,
Our mother! first and last.

• • •

The New Year

Here's to the bright New Year
And a fond farewell to the old;
Here's to the things that are yet to come
And the memories that we hold.

May the New Year bring summer in its wake.

—IRISH

May all your troubles during the coming year
be as short-lived as your New Year's resolutions.

As we start the New Year,
Let's get down on our knees
To thank God we're on our feet.

Here's to you a New Year's toast
May your joy ne'er see a sorrow's ghost.

In the New Year,
May your right hand always
be stretched out in friendship,
and never in want.

—IRISH

In the year ahead,
May we treat our friends with kindness and
our enemies with generosity.

Let us resolve to do the best we can
with what we've got.

—WILLIAM FEATHER

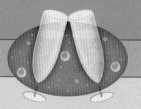

A Vintage Toast

To Forgetting

'Tis better to forget,
than remember with regret.

. . .

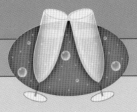

A Vintage Toast

To Our
Illustrious Dead

Over their hallowed graves,
may the winds of heaven whisper
hourly benedictions.

. . .

May it be the best year yet for you
And everything prosper you may do.

May the best of this year be the worst of next.

Here's to the present—
and to hell with the past!
A health to the future and joy to the last!

May the Lord keep you in his hand
and never close his fist too tight on you.

May your nets be always full—
your pockets never empty.
May your horse not cast a shoe
nor the devil look at you
in the coming year.

The Old Man's dead. He was okay, maybe
But here's a health to the brand-new baby.
I give you 20__.

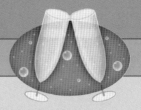

A Vintage Toast

To Long Ago

Old-fashioned songs,
And old-fashioned weather;
Old-fashioned books,
And old-fashioned leather;
Old-fashioned girls,
And mothers and boys;
A toast, each and all,
To old-fashioned joys.

. . .

To a firm hand for a flighty beast,
an old dog for the long road,
a kettle of fish for Friday,
and a welcome for the New Year.

—IRISH

Welcome be ye that are here,
Welcome all, and make good cheer,
Welcome all, another year.

．　．　．

Parents

We raise a glass to those who raised us.

To Mother and Dad on their wedding
anniversary;
We never know the love of our parents for us
till we become parents.
—HENRY WARD BEECHER

To the new parents,
Who are about to enter a "changing" world.

Here's to my parents:
Two people who spent half their life
wondering how I'd turn out, and the rest of the
time when I'd turn in!

To my parents,
who have spoiled me my whole life long:
Don't stop!

. . .

Professions

ACCOUNTANTS

To my accountant:
May he make brilliant deductions.

Let's have a toast to the most calculating
person we know!

ARCHITECTS

Here's to the ivy,
That eventually covers our mistakes.

To the architect, one who drafts
a plan of your house,
And plans a draft of your money.

ARTISTS

May you be hung!

May the critics be kind.

BANKERS

To our friend the banker,
May he never lose interest.

BLACKSMITHS

Here's a success to forgery.

BUILDERS

Drinks are on the house,
So someone get a ladder!

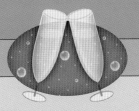

A Vintage Toast

To the Fool

Generally the wisest man in
the company, disguised.

. . .

Here's to the carpenter,
He came, he sawed, and he fixed it!

Here's to the man who comes home every day,
And says his work was riveting.

COACHES

Here's to our coach, a man [woman] who's
willing to lay down our lives
For his [her] school.

CRITICS

To the critic,
Someone who likes to write,
About things he doesn't like.

DENTISTS

To the dentist,
who makes his living hand to mouth.

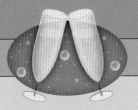

A Vintage Toast

To Money

The finest linguist in the world.

. . .

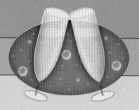

A Vintage Toast

To Pen and Pencil

Twin conquerors,
greater than Alexander.

. . .

Here's to the dentist who got most of his
training in the military,
As a drill sergeant!

DIPLOMATS

Here's to the diplomat,
Whose speciality is letting you have
her (his) way.

To the diplomat, a person who
can tell a man to go to hell
In such a way that he'll look forward
to making the trip!

To the diplomat,
A person who is held upright
By equal pressure from all directions.

To the diplomat, an ex-politician
Who has mastered the art of holding
his tongue.

To the diplomat and diplomacy,
Which Ambrose Bierce defined as
The patriotic art of lying for one's country.

DOCTORS

Here's to good doctors,
They add life to your years,
Rather than years to your life!

JOURNALISTS

Here's to the press—
The "tongue" of the country,
may it never be cut out.

LAWYERS

Here's to my lawyer, a man of great trials
And many convictions.

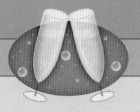

A Vintage Toast

To Ambition

Let us keep our eyes on the stars though
our soles be in the mud.

. . .

A Vintage Toast

To Our Political Foes

Here's that they may soon be converted
to our way of thinking.

. . .

Here's to the lawyer, a bright gentleman,
Who rescues your estate from your enemies,
And keeps it for himself.

To Lawyers—
You cannot live without the lawyers,
and certainly you cannot die without them.
—JOSEPH H. CHOATE

POLITICIANS

Here's to the politician,
a person who divides his time
Between running for office
and running for cover.

Here's to the politician,
a person who straddles the issue
When he isn't dodging one.

Here's to the honest politician—a man who
when bought stays bought.

PSYCHIATRISTS

To psychiatrists,
They find you cracked,
And leave you broke.

To the psychiatrist,
A person who doesn't have to worry
As long as other people do.

STOCKBROKERS

Here's to the stockbroker,
He can tell you what's going to happen
next month to your money
And later explain why it didn't.

Here's to the stockbroker,
May your life be full of bulls!

. . .

St. Patrick's Day

May the Irish hills caress you.
May her lakes and rivers bless you.
May the luck of the Irish enfold you.
May the blessings of St. Patrick behold you.

The anniversary of St. Patrick's day—and may
the Shamrock be green forever.

St. Patrick was a gentleman
Who through strategy and stealth
Drove all the snakes from Ireland,
Here's a toasting to his health;
But not too many toastings
Lest you lose yourself and then
Forget the good St. Patrick
And see all those snakes again.

—IRISH

. . .

Thanksgiving

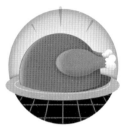

May our pleasures be boundless while
we have time to enjoy them.

Let us toast to our blessings and good fortune
on this Thanksgiving Day.

Here's to the blessings of the year,
Here's to the friends we hold so dear,
To peace on earth, both far and near.

Here's to the day when the Yankees
first acknowledge
Heaven's good gifts with Thank'ees.

Here's to the good old turkey,
The bird that comes each fall,
And with his sweet persuasive meat
Makes gobblers of us all.

To our national birds—
The American Eagle,
The Thanksgiving Turkey:
May one give us peace in all our States—
And the other a piece for all our plates.

. . .

Weddings

A toast to love and laughter
and happily ever after.

To the bride and groom:
May all their troubles be little ones.

Look down you gods,
And on this couple drop a blessed crown.

—WILLIAM SHAKESPEARE

May those who enter the rosy paths of
matrimony never meet with thorns.

To the bride and groom—
May they have a lifetime of love and
an eternity of happiness.

Happiness to the newlyweds
from the oldyweds.

To the bride and groom:
May their joys be as deep as the ocean,
And their misfortune as light as its foam.

Here is to the bride:
May your hours of joy be as numerous as
the petals of your bridal bouquet.

May your voyage through life be
as happy and as free
As the dancing waves on the deep blue sea.

By all means marry; if you get a good wife,
You'll become happy; if you get a bad one,
You'll become a philosopher.

—SOCRATES

May you be poor in misfortune,
Rich in blessings,
Slow to make enemies,
Quick to make friends.
But rich or poor, quick or slow,
May you know nothing but happiness
From this day forward.

—IRISH

Heaven give thee many, many merry days.

—WILLIAM SHAKESPEARE

May the most you wish for be the least you get.

To the two secrets to a long-lasting
happy marriage:
Here's to a good sense of humor and
a short memory!

Let us celebrate this occasion
with wine and sweet words.
—LATIN PROVERB

It is written:
"When children find true love,
parents find true joy."
Here's to your joy and ours,
from this day forward.
—PARENTS' TOAST TO THEIR CHILDREN

With trumpets and fanfare,
I wish you the happiest of all days.

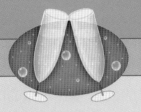

A Vintage Toast

To the
American Beauty

May she be ever, as now,
Queen Rose of the World.

. . .

Let us toast the health of the bride,
Let us toast the health of the groom,
Let us toast the person that tied,
Let us toast every guest in the room.

May their joys be as bright as the morning,
and their sorrows but shadows that fade
in the sunlight of love.

May we all live to be present at their
Golden Wedding.

May your love be as endless
as your wedding rings.

May you be merry and lack nothing.

—WILLIAM SHAKESPEARE

May you have enough happiness to
keep you sweet;
enough trials to keep you strong;
enough sorrow to keep you human;
enough hope to keep you happy;
enough failure to keep you humble;
enough success to keep you eager;
enough friends to give you comfort;
enough faith and courage in yourself, your
business, and your country to
banish depression;
enough wealth to meet your needs;
enough determination to make each day a
better day than yesterday.

To the newlyweds: May "for better or worse"
be far better than worse.

To the bride and groom:
May your wedding days be few and your
anniversaries many.

Grow old with me!
The best is yet to be,
The last of life,
For which, the first is made.

—ROBERT BROWNING

Here's to my mother-in-law's daughter,
Here's to her father-in-law's son;
And here's to the vows we've just taken,
And the life we've just begun.

Here's to thee and thy folks
from me and my folks;
And if thee and thy folks love me and my folks
As much as me and my folks
love thee and thy folks,
Then there never was folks
since folks was folks
Love me and my folks as much
as thee and thy folks.

Here's to the Bride and the Groom!
May you have a happy honeymoon,
May you lead a happy life,
May you have a bunch of money soon,
And live without all strife.

Here's to the bride that is to be,
Here's to the groom she'll wed,
May all their troubles be light as bubbles
Or the feathers that make up their bed!

Here's to the groom with bride so fair,
And here's to the bride with groom so rare!

Here's to the happy man:
All mankind love a lover.
—RALPH WALDO EMERSON

Here's to the husband—and here's to the wife;
May they remain lovers for the rest
of their life.

Down the hatch to a striking match!

Here's to the bride and mother-in-law,
Here's to the groom and father-in-law,
Here's to sister and brother-in-law,
Here's to friends and friends-in-law,
May none of them need an attorney-at-law.

May your marriage be like a fine wine,
    Getting better and better with age.

• • •

Wine

To clean glasses and old corks.

Drink wine, and live here blitheful
while ye may;
The morrow's life too late is,—live today!

Here's to mine and here's to thine!
Now's the time to clink it!
Here's a flagon of old wine,
And here we are to drink it.

—RICHARD HOVEY

Here's to the man
Who owns the land
That bears the grapes
That makes the wine
That tastes as good
As this does.

Here's to water, water divine—
It dews the grapes that give us wine.

Then a smile, and a glass,
and a toast and a cheer,
For all the good wine,
and we've some of it here.

—OLIVER WENDELL HOLMES

To the big-bellied bottle.

When wine enlivens the heart
May friendship surround the table.

Wine and women—
May we always have a taste for both.

One barrel of wine can work more miracles
than a church full of saints.
—ITALIAN PROVERB

May friendship, like wine,
improve as time advances,
And may we always have old wine,
old friends, and young cares.

May your love be like good wine, and grow
stronger as it grows older.
—OLD ENGLISH TOAST

May our wine brighten the rays of friendship,
but never diminish its luster.

May our wine brighten the mind and
strengthen the resolution.

With each glass of this wine, I double the
number of friends I have in this room.

Here's to the heart that fills as
the wine bottle empties.

May we never want for wine,
nor for a friend to help drink it.

To you, and yours, and theirs, and mine,
I pledge with you, their health in wine.

Here's to our next joyous meeting—
and, oh, when we meet,
May our wine be as bright and
our union as sweet.

Here's to the triple alliance—Friendship,
Freedom, and Wine.

Give me wine to wash me clean
From the weather-stains of care.
—RALPH WALDO EMERSON

To Wine:
It improves with age—I like it more
the older I get.

A bottle of wine contains more philosophy
than all the books in the world.
—LOUIS PASTEUR

. . .

Wives

To my wife: my bride and joy.

Here's to the lovely woman
I fought to marry at any cost,
The struggle was worth it,
without her I'd be lost.

Here's a toast to those who make toasts
worthwhile—Our Wives!

Here's to our better halves,
Who reconcile us to our poorer quarters!

A good wife and health,
Are a man's best wealth.

A thing of beauty is a joy forever.
Here's to you, my beautiful bride.

—JOHN KEATS

A health to our widows,
If they ever marry again, may they do as well!

To my wife and our anniversary,
Which I forgot once but never will again!

Here's looking at you, dear!
Though I should pour a sea of wine,
My eyes would thirst for more.

To my wife,
Here's to the prettiest, here's to the wittiest,
Here's to the truest of all who are true,
Here's to the neatest one, here's
to the sweetest one,
Here's to them all in one—here's to you.

.   .   .

Women

Who loves not women, wine and song,
Remains a fool his whole life long.

—JOHN HENRY VOSS

To woman,
A paradox who puzzles when she pleases
and pleases when she puzzles.

Here's to Woman—who generally speaking
is generally speaking.

Here's to Woman—once our superior,
now our equal.

A wise woman puts a grain of sugar into
Everything she says to a man,
And she takes a grain of salt
With everything he says to her.

Drink to fair woman, who, I think,
Is most entitled to it,
For if anything can drive me to drink,
She certainly could do it.

Here's to women: they're the loveliest flowers
that bloom under heaven.

To the ladies, God bless them,
May nothing distress them.

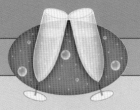

A Vintage Toast

To the Clever Woman

Clever enough to convince us that we are
cleverer than she at her cleverest.

. . .

Woman's faults are many
Men have only two;
Everything they say,
And everything they do.

As for the women,
though we scorn and flout 'em,
We may live with, but cannot live without 'em.

To the girl we love! When she is our toast
we don't want any but her.

. . .

Good day,
good health,
good cheer,
good night!

.   .   .

Bibliography

Antrim, Minna Thomas. *A Book of Toasts*. Philadelphia, Pennsylvania: Henry Altemus Company, 1902.

Bridges, John and Bryan Curtis. *A Gentleman Raises His Glass: A Concise, Contemporary Guide to the Noble Tradition of the Toast*. Nashville, Tennessee: Rutledge Hills Press, 2003.

Conover, Jennifer Rahel. *Toasts for Every Occasion: Warm, Wise, and Witty Words Collected from Around the World*. New York, New York: New American Library, 2001.

Dickson, Paul. *Toasts: Over 1,500 of the Best Toasts, Sentiments, Blessings, and Graces*. New York, New York: Crown Publishers, Inc., 1981.

Evans III, William R. and Andrew Frothingham. *Crisp Toasts: Wonderful Words That Add Wit and Class Every Time You Raise Your Glass*. New York, New York: St. Martin's Press, 1992.

Garrison, Robert L. *Here's to You! 354 Toasts You Can Use Today for Parties, Holidays, and Public Affairs.* New York, New York: Crown Publishers, Inc., 1980.

Henry, Lewis C. *Toasts for All Occasions*. Garden City, New Jersey: Doubleday & Co., Inc, Garden City Books, 1949.

Irish Toasts. San Francisco: Chronicle Books LLC, 1987.

John, Justin and Kaplan Bartlett. *Bartlett's Familiar Quotations: A Collection of Passages, Phrases, and Proverbs Traced to Their Sources in Ancient and Modern Literature*. 17th ed. New York, New York: Little, Brown & Company, 2002.

McNutt, Joni G. *In Praise of Wine: An Offering of Hearty Toasts, Quotations, Witticisms, Proverbs and Poetry Throughout History*. Santa Barbara, California: Capra Press, 1993.

Noel, Darren. *Pocket Guide to Wedding Speeches & Toasts*. London, England: PRC Publishing Ltd., 2003.

Post, Elizabeth L. *Emily Post's Complete Book of Wedding Etiquette*, Revised Edition. New York, New York: Harper-Collins Publishers, 1991.

Index